SNCF WORKSHOPS, DEPOTS AND YARDS

MARTIN BRAY

AMBERLEY

About the Author

My interest in railways started at the age of six when my father used to drop me off on his way to work at the level crossing near Bognor Regis railway station. My passion for railways led me into an engineering apprenticeship with one of the most respected manufacturers of railway locomotives, Ruston Diesels Limited, in 1973. My interest in SNCF began with a motorcycle trip to Paris, Dijon and Lyon in 1982 and more than forty years later I am the proud photographer of one of the best collections of SNCF diesel and electric locomotive photographs. My retirement in December 2019 has enabled me to spend more time photographing the decline of diesel and electric locomotives in France and landscape photography in the Canary Islands.

Front cover: Chambéry depot's iconic, fully enclosed roundhouse with glass dome, 5 June 2024.

First published 2025

Amberley Publishing
The Hill, Stroud
Gloucestershire, GL5 4EP

www.amberley-books.com

ISBN 978 1 3981 2046 4 (print)
ISBN 978 1 3981 2047 1 (ebook)

British Library Cataloguing in Publication Data.
A catalogue record for this book is available from the British Library.

Origination by Amberley Publishing.
Printed in the UK.

Appointed GPSR EU Representative:
Easy Access System Europe Oü, 16879218
Address: Mustamäe tee 50, 10621, Tallinn, Estonia
Contact Details: gpsr.requests@easproject.com, +358 40 500 3575

Introduction

SNCF was formed in 1938 with the nationalisation of Est, État, Nord, PLM, PO-Midi, Alsace-Lorraine and Great Little Belt railway companies. During the formation of SNCF some of the network to the south of Paris was already electrified at 1,500V direct current. During the modernisation programme of the railways in 1955, the network to the north of Paris was electrified to the new standard of 25,000V alternating current.

SNCF has made significant investment in new high-technology passenger trains and it is anticipated that the remaining locomotive-hauled passenger trains will be withdrawn by 2026. There are four remaining diesel locomotive-hauled passenger trains and the last strongholds for electric locomotive-hauled passenger trains are out of Paris Austerlitz /Nord/Saint Lazare, Lyon, Lille and between Bordeaux and Marseille.

SNCF has withdrawn its loss-making wagon load traffic business and some of its more lucrative freight contracts have been taken over by the private sector. This and new investment in locomotives have resulted in a large reduction in the fleet of electric, diesel and diesel shunting locomotives.

The reduction in electric, diesel and diesel shunting locomotives in both the passenger and freight sectors and the construction of new purpose-built workshops and depots for new-technology rolling stock has resulted in the closure of many workshops and depots throughout SNCF.

The withdrawal of wagon load traffic, loss of lucrative freight flows and the increase in block freight trains have reduced the demand for reforming, and as a result of this many marshalling yards have closed and others are operating with low volumes of traffic.

SNCF Fret is currently being restructured into two new companies, Hexafret and Technis, as a result of a European Commission investigation into €5.3 billion of illegal aid given to the company between 2007 and 2019. The restructure will become effective on 1 January 2025 and during the transition SNCF Fret will be handing over twenty-three mostly intermodal services to the private sector, together with a 'suggested' fifty locomotives and several hundred members of staff, resulting in a 30 per cent reduction in traffic (tonne-kilometres) and a 20 per cent reduction in turnover. Around 3,900 employees are to be automatically transferred to New Fret and 500 to New Maintenance.

(Note: Workshops, depots and yards specifically refers to electric, diesel and diesel shunting locomotives and not to electric and diesel multiple units.)

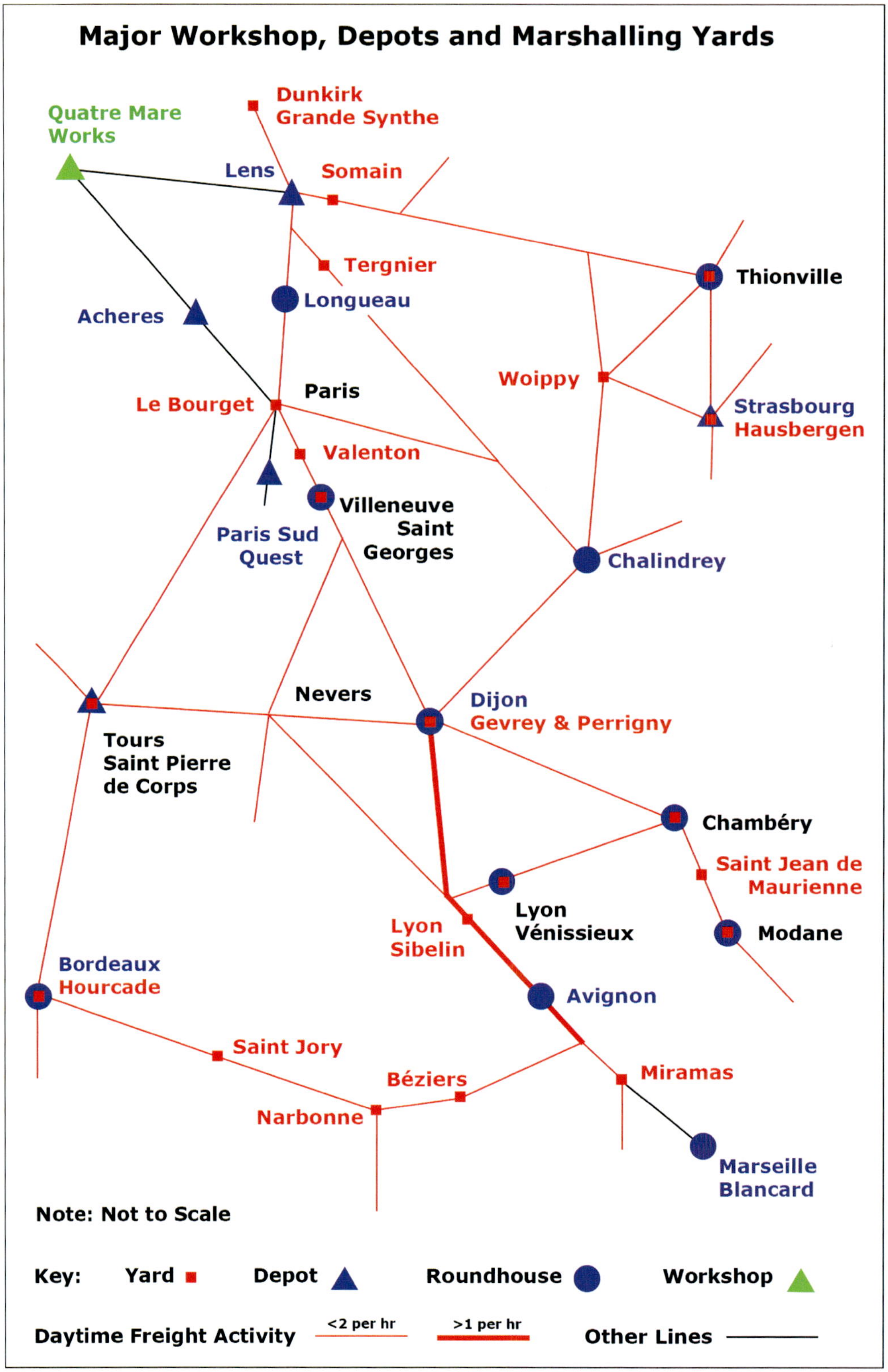
Major Workshop, Depots and Marshalling Yards
Quatre Mare Works
Dunkirk Grande Synthe
Lens
Somain
Tergnier
Thionville
Longueau
Acheres
Woippy
Paris
Le Bourget
Strasbourg Hausbergen
Valenton
Villeneuve Saint Georges
Paris Sud Quest
Chalindrey
Nevers
Dijon
Gevrey & Perrigny
Tours Saint Pierre de Corps
Chambéry
Saint Jean de Maurienne
Lyon Vénissieux
Modane
Lyon Sibelin
Bordeaux Hourcade
Avignon
Saint Jory
Béziers
Miramas
Narbonne
Marseille Blancard
Note: Not to Scale
Key: Yard Depot Roundhouse Workshop
Daytime Freight Activity <2 per hr >1 per hr
Other Lines

The map opposite illustrates the geographical layout of SNCF's major workshop, depots and yards relating to diesel and electric locomotives in France and is not to scale.

Workshop and depots are shown before the restructure.

Quatre Mares (Sotteville) is the only workshop that is now open for the overhaul and refurbishment of diesel and electric locomotives, although many of the other depots do undertake some types of heavy repair work.

Locomotives, electric and diesel multiple units and carriages are not specifically allocated to depots but are the responsibility of the Technical Fleet Supervision (STF) of the region, activity or third party, where they would normally be operating. However, infrastructure locomotives are normally maintained at Chalindrey or Longeau and Fret to most of the other depots.

Locomotives and other types of rolling stock are currently being scrapped in a disused yard opposite Baroncourt station between Metz and Longuyon.

Only the major marshalling yards are shown together with an indication of the daytime level of freight activity between locations, which includes privately operated freight. Usually container (intermodal) and dedicated company trains would only use the yards for either recessing or crew changes.

Whilst wagonload traffic was virtually eliminated twenty years ago, lengthy mixed freight trains often with locomotives (dead in tow) are still operating between Sibelin (Lyon) and Woippy (Metz) yards. Hump shunting is still being undertaken on a limited basis at Woippy, Le Bourget and Sibelin yards with BB64700 and BB64800 diesel locomotives. Many yards throughout France are being used to store withdrawn rolling stock.

The busiest freight corridor during the day appears to be between north of Sibelin (Lyon) yard, where the line diverges towards Nevers, Dijon and Chambéry and south of Avignon, where the lines diverge to Miramas (Marseille) yard and Béziers. Much of the freight on this stretch of line is international container (intermodal) traffic operating between France, Belgium, Luxembourg, Germany, Switzerland, Italy and Spain.

From a photography perspective, Rue Paul Descartes, 1 km south of Saint Fons station, is an excellent location adjacent to the line without fencing for snapping in the mornings. In the afternoons the road overbridge at the north end of Saint Fons station is almost as good. When it's raining the centre island platform at Saint Fons station captures all the freight and passenger trains north of Sibelin (Lyon) yard.

One of the most picturesque locations in France for photography is the Maurienne line between Chambéry and Modane in the Rhone Alps, where snow may be seen on the peaks as late as May. It's a very tortuous route in terms of both inclines and curvature and here many freight trains require banking from Saint Jean de Maurienne to Modane. Modane has a small quarter roundhouse and is the border town with Italy, where most freight trains change locomotives. The 'Rolling Highway' train conveying lorries between Aiten (Chambéry) and Orbassano (Italy) passes along this line and is rostered for pairs of Astride BB36300 locomotives throughout. The route is currently closed following a major landslide during August 2022 at Saint Michel de Maurienne and is expected to reopen during 2024.

2D2 5525 was built by CEM Fives during 1934. It is pictured in green livery at Paris Montrouge depot on 15 May 1992 and was withdrawn from service during 1980 for preservation.

2D2 9135 was built by CEM Fives during 1951. It is pictured in green livery at Paris Charolais depot on 15 May 1992 and was withdrawn from service during 1987 for preservation.

A1A A1A 62049 was built by Baldwin Locomotive Works during 1946. It is pictured in green livery at Lens depot on 27 October 1991 and was withdrawn from service during 1990.

A1A A1A 62062 was built by Baldwin Locomotive Works during 1947. It is pictured in green livery at Thionville depot on 14 November 1994 and was withdrawn from service during 1993.

A1A A1A 68046 was built by CAFL/CEM Fives during 1966. It is pictured in blue livery at Châlons sur Marne depot on 13 November 1994 and was withdrawn from service during 2004.

A1A A1A 68526 was built by CAFL/CEM/SACM Fives during 1967. It is pictured in blue livery at Chalindrey depot and was withdrawn from service during 2004.

Several Class 71000 diesel locomotives are shown in the closed Autun depot on 28 July 1982. The line north of Autun to Avallon was privatised for freight traffic and operated by CFD using four ex-British Rail Class 20 locomotives during the 1990s.

BB322 was built by Alsthom during 1938. It is pictured in green livery at Paris Sud Ouest depot on 15 May 1992 and was withdrawn from service during 1997.

BB327 was built by Alsthom during 1946. It is pictured in primer at Miramas depot on 9 April 2014 and was withdrawn from service during 1997 for preservation.

BB354 was built by Alsthom during 1948. It is pictured in green livery at Paris Charolais depot on 15 May 1992 and was withdrawn from service during 1996.

BB4152 was built by CEF Alstom during 1930. It is pictured in green livery at Béziers workshops on 29 July 1987 and had been withdrawn from service the previous year.

BB4754 was built by CEF Alsthom during 1934. It is pictured in green livery undergoing wheelset attention at Paris Sud Ouest depot on 15 May 1992 and was withdrawn from service during 1993.

BB4764 was built by CEF Alsthom during 1935. It is pictured in green livery being shunted on the traverser at Paris Sud Ouest depot on 15 May 1992 and was withdrawn from service during 1993.

BB7279 was built by Alsthom/MTE during 1979. It is pictured in grey livery undergoing maintenance at Paris Sud Ouest depot on 16 November 1994 and was withdrawn from service during 2015.

BB7323 was built by Alsthom/MTE during 1981 and is pictured in grey livery on the turntable at Paris Charolais depot on 26 October 1991.

BB7400 was built by Alshtom/MTE during 1982. It is pictured in FRET green livery at Toulouse depot on 3 July 2015 and was withdrawn from service during 2018.

BB7408 was built by Alsthom/MTE during 1983. It is pictured in grey livery at Toulouse depot on 16 September 2015 and was withdrawn from service during 2016.

BB7419 was built by Alstom/MTE during 1984. It is pictured in grey livery at Dijon Perrigny depot on 5 September 2014 and was withdrawn from service during 2015.

BB7435 was built by Alsthom MTE during 1985. It is pictured in grey livery whilst on test at Oullins workshops on 30 July 1987 and was withdrawn from service during 2019.

BB8139 was built by Alsthom during 1950. It is pictured in green livery at Paris Charolais depot on 15 May 1992 and was withdrawn from service during 2009 after being renumbered BB80005 in 1996 for empty coaching stock movements in Paris.

BB8177 was built by Alsthom during 1952. It is pictured in weathered green livery at Miramas depot on 9 April 2014 and was withdrawn from service during 1999 for preservation.

BB8239 was built by Alsthom during 1953. It is pictured during overhaul at Béziers workshops on 29 July 1987 and was withdrawn from service during 1997.

BB8257 was built by Alstom during 1954. It is pictured undergoing maintenance at Paris Sud Ouest depot on 16 November 1994 and was withdrawn from service during 2004.

BB8617 was built by Alsthom during 1974. It is pictured in En Voyage livery beside the traverser at Toulouse depot on 3 July 2015 and was withdrawn from service during 2015.

BB9250 was built by Schneider-Jeaumont during 1959. It is pictured in green livery undergoing overhaul at Oullins works on 30 July 1987 and was withdrawn from service during 2004.

BB9264 was built by Schneider-Jeaumont during 1959. It is pictured in grey livery at Villeneuve Saint Georges depot on 18 May 1995 and was withdrawn from service during 2006.

BB9301 was built by Schneider-Jeaumont during 1967. It is pictured in multiserve livery at Toulouse depot on 22 May 2012 and was withdrawn from service during 2014.

BB9437 was built by Fives/MTE during 1961. It is pictured in Arzens livery at Béziers works on 29 July 1987 and has been withdrawn from service.

BB12032 was built by Alsthom during 1957. It is pictured in green livery at Aulnoye-Aymeries depot on 17 November 1994 and was withdrawn from service during 1999.

BB12036 was built by Alsthom during 1957. It is pictured in green livery at Mohon depot on 17 November 1994 and was withdrawn from service earlier that year.

BB12113 was built by Alsthom during 1960. It is pictured in green livery at Lens depot on 18 November 1994 and was withdrawn from service during 1998.

BB12120 was built by Alsthom during 1960. It is pictured in green livery at Paris Le Bourget yard on 16 May 1992 and was withdrawn from service during 1993.

BB13052 was built by MTE/Fives during 1957. It is pictured in green livery at the former Strasbourg Hausbergen yard depot on 14 November 1994 and was withdrawn from service during 1994 for preservation.

BB15062 was built by Alsthom/MTE during 1978 and is pictured in TEE livery at Paris La Villette depot on 15 May 1992.

BB15064 was built by Alstom/MTE during 1978 and is pictured in TEE livery at Thionville depot on 14 November 1994.

BB16051 was built by MTE during 1961. It is pictured in grey livery on the traverser at Paris La Chapelle depot on 15 May 1992 and was withdrawn from service during 2012.

BB16578 was built by Alsthom during 1961. It is pictured in grey livery at Paris La Villette depot on 15 May 1992 and was withdrawn from service during 2004.

BB16608 was built by Alsthom during 1961. It is pictured in grey livery at Metz Woippy yard on 15 November 1994 and was withdrawn from service during 2003.

BB16769 was built by Alsthom during 1964. It is pictured in grey livery at Paris Le Bourget yard on 16 May 1992 and was withdrawn from service during 2008.

BB16788 was built by Alsthom during 1964. It is pictured in grey livery at Thionville depot on 14 November 1994 and was withdrawn from service during 2006.

BB17002 was built by Alsthom during 1965. It is pictured in grey livery at Châlons sur Marne depot on 13 November 1994 and was withdrawn from service during 2015.

BB17034 was built by Alsthom during 1966. It is pictured in grey livery at Achères depot on 26 October 1991 and was withdrawn from service during 2013.

BB17090 was built by Alsthom during 1968. It is pictured in grey livery at Paris La Chapelle depot on 15 May 1992 and was withdrawn from service during 2017.

BB22223 was built by Alsthom during 1977 and is pictured in Transilien livery on the turntable at Villeneuve Saint Georges depot on 17 April 2015.

BB22330 was built by Alsthom during 1980 and is pictured in grey livery at Marseille Saint Charles depot on 24 May 2013.

BB22350 was built by Alsthom during 1980 and is pictured in En Voyage livery at Chambéry depot on 2 September 2014.

BB22375 was built by Alsthom during 1983 and is pictured in grey livery at Strasbourg depot on 26 August 2019.

BB22380 was built by Alsthom during 1984 and is pictured in Infra livery at Villeneuve Saint Georges depot on 17 April 2015.

BB25230 was built by MTE during 1966. It is pictured in green livery at Achères depot on 16 May 1992 and was withdrawn from service during 2005.

BB25527 was built by Alsthom during 1965. It is pictured in grey livery at Achères depot on 26 October 1991 and was withdrawn from service during 2005.

BB25580 was built by Alsthom during 1972. It is pictured in grey livery at Villeneuve Saint Georges depot on 18 May 1995 and was withdrawn from service during 2004.

BB25679 was built by Alsthom during 1975. It is pictured in green livery at Lyon Vénissieux depot on 30 July 1987 and was withdrawn from service during 2021.

BB26059 was built by Alsthom during 1991 and is pictured in grey livery at Forbach depot on 14 November 1994.

BB26113 was built by Alsthom during 1993 and is pictured in grey livery at Modane depot on 3 September 2014.

BB26159 was built by Alsthom during 1994 and is pictured in grey livery at Strasbourg depot on 28 July 2019.

BB27005 was built by Alsthom during 2001 and is pictured at Tours Saint Pierre de Corps yard on 1 July 2016.

BB27019 was built by Alsthom during 2002 and is pictured at Metz Woippy yard stabling point on 28 August 2019.

BB27019 was built by Alsthom during 2002 and is pictured passing through Metz Woippy yard on 28 August 2019.

BB36355 was built by GEC-Alsthom during 2001 and is pictured at Modane depot on 3 September 2014.

BB37052 was built by Alsthom during 2006 and is pictured at Metz Woippy yard stabling point on 10 April 2019.

BB60038 was built by Alsthom/Vossloh during 2008 and is pictured at Villeneuve Saint Georges depot on 17 April 2015.

BB60133 was built by Alsthom/Vossloh during 2009 and is pictured at Strasbourg Hausbergen yard stabling point on 10 May 2022.

BB62413 was built by Alsthom during 1954 for Belgian Railways and seconded to SNCF during 1990 for Channel Tunnel and TGV construction traffic. It is pictured in blue livery at Longueau depot on 17 May 1992 and has subsequently been returned to Belgian Railways.

BB63083 was built by Brissonneau & Lotz during 1956. It is pictured in green livery at Paris Sud Ouest depot on 15 May 1992 and was withdrawn from service during 1993.

BB63766 was built by Brissonneau & Lotz during 1961. It is pictured in green livery at Lens depot on 18 November 1994 and was withdrawn from service during 2005.

BB63826 was built by Brissonneau & Lotz during 1962. It is pictured in green livery at Paris La Plaine depot on 16 May 1992 and was withdrawn from service during 2008.

BB63992 was built by Brissonneau & Lotz during 1968. It is pictured in green livery at Lyon Vénissieux depot on 30 July 1987 and was withdrawn from service to be re-engineered into BB64608.

BB64711 and BB64811, formerly BB63874 and BB63022, were built by Brissonneau & Lotz during 1967 and 1954, respectively, and converted to a master-and-slave unit for shunting in marshalling yards. It is pictured in orange and brown livery at Strasbourg Hausbergen yard on 14 November 1994.

BB64717 and BB64817, formerly BB63937 and BB63047, were built by Brissonneau & Lotz during 1966 and 1955, respectively, and converted to a master-and-slave unit for shunting in marshalling yards. It is pictured in orange and brown livery at Somaine Yard on 18 November 1994 and was withdrawn from service during 2021.

BB64809 and BB64709, formerly BB63051 and BB63946, were built by Brissonneau & Lotz during 1955 and 1966, respectively, and converted to a master-and-slave unit for shunting in marshalling yards. It is pictured in orange and brown livery at Metz Woippy yard on 15 November 1994.

BB66126 was built by CAFL/CEM/Alsthom/Fives-Lille/SACM during 1963. It is pictured in blue livery at Chalindrey depot on 16 April 2015 and was withdrawn from service during 2016.

BB66265 was built by CAFL/CEM/Alsthom/Fives-Lille/SACM during 1966. It is pictured in blue livery at Lyon Vénissieux depot on 30 July 1987 and was withdrawn from service during 2021.

BB66277 was built by CAFL/CEM/Alsthom/Fives-Lille/SACM during 1967. It is pictured in blue livery at Longueau depot on 17 May 1992 and was withdrawn from service during 2015.

BB66447 was built by CAFL/CEM/Alsthom/Fives-Lille/SACM during 1969 and is pictured in blue livery at Paris Le Bourget yard on 16 May 1992.

BB66447 was built by CAFL/CEM/Alsthom/Fives-Lille/SACM during 1969 and is pictured in blue livery at Mohon depot on 17 November 1994.

BB67212 was built by Brissonneau & Lotz/MTE during 1967 and is pictured in blue livery at Chalindrey depot on 16 April 2015.

BB67235 was built by Brissonneau & Lotz/MTE during 1964 and is pictured in blue livery at Nevers depot on 14 January 2017.

BB67256 was built by Brissonneau & Lotz/MTE during 1966 and is pictured in blue livery departing Nevers depot on 11 October 2021 in a consist of thirteen locomotives bound for Chalindrey depot.

BB67279 was built by Brissonneau & Lotz/MTE during 1964 and is pictured in blue livery at Strasbourg Hausbergen yard on 10 May 2022.

BB67305 was built by Brissonneau & Lotz/MTE during 1968. It is pictured in blue livery at Chambéry depot and withdrawn from service during 2017.

BB67329 was built by Brissonneau & Lotz/MTE during 1968. It is pictured in blue livery at Villeneuve Saint Georges depot on 16 May 1992 and was withdrawn from service during 2010.

BB67373 was built by Brissonneau & Lotz/MTE during 1967. It is pictured in Isobel livery at Chambéry depot on 2 September 2014 and was withdrawn from service during 2011.

BB67406 was built by Brissonneau & Lotz/MTE during 1970 and is pictured in En Voyage livery at Nevers depot on 10 October 2021. The BB67400 locomotive is the maid for all types of traction including freight, infrastructure, passenger and rescue locomotives for TGVs. They are also occasionally seen on the Venice Simplon Orient Express.

BB67456 was built by Brissonneau & Lotz/MTE during 1971 and is pictured in blue livery at Nevers depot on 14 January 2017.

BB67618 was built by Brissonneau & Lotz/MTE during 1975. It is pictured in blue livery at Amiens depot on 17 May 1992 and was withdrawn from service during 2012.

BB69290 was built by CAFL/CEM/Alsthom/Fives-Lille/SACM during 1967 and is pictured in Infra livery at Nevers depot on 14 July 2017.

BB69311 was built by CAFL/CEM/Alsthom/Fives-Lille/SACM during 1967. It is pictured in Fret livery at Dijon depot on 5 September 2014 and was withdrawn from service during 2015.

BB69315 was built by CAFL/CEM/Alsthom/Fives-Lille/SACM during 1968 and is pictured in blue livery at Toulouse depot on 16 September 2015.

BB75124 was built by Alsthom/Siemens during 2009 and is pictured in Fret livery at Strasbourg Hausbergen yard on 10 May 2022.

BB75124 was built by Alsthom/Siemens during 2009 and is pictured in Fret livery at Strasbourg Hausbergen yard on 25 April 2018.

BB79021 was built by Vossloh during 2021. It is pictured in Infra livery at Nevers depot on 10 October 2021.

BB80004, formerly BB8247, was built by Alsthom/Schneider/Jeaumont during 1954. It is pictured in grey livery at Villeneuve Saint Georges yard and had been withdrawn from service by 2010.

In the foreground are several lines of withdrawn diesel shunting locomotives (Y7000 and Y8000) at the rear of the former workshops at Béziers. In the background are several shunting locomotives (Y8000 and Y900) at the stabling point. Picture taken on 7 September 2014.

Several BB8500 and BB9400 locomotives are awaiting overhaul at the rear of Béziers workshops on 29 July 1987.

A selection of BB7200 and BB67400 locomotives at Bordeaux depot on 23 May 2013.

CC1101 was built by CGC/Oerlikon during 1938. It is pictured in green livery at Béziers workshops on 29 July 1987 and was withdrawn from service during 2003.

CC1107 was built by CGC/Oerlikon during 1945. It is pictured in green livery at Villeneuve Saint Georges depot on 16 May 1992 and was withdrawn from service during 2005.

CC6509 was built by Alsthom/MTE during 1969. It is pictured in TEE livery at Lyon Oullins workshops on 30 July 1987 and was withdrawn from service during 2004.

CC6531 was built by Alsthom/MTE during 1971. It is pictured in TEE livery at Paris Charolais depot on 15 May 1992 and was withdrawn from service during 2004.

CC6543 was built by Alsthom/MTE during 1971. It is pictured in blue/green livery at Villeneuve Saint Georges depot on 16 November 1994 and withdrawn from service during 2004. CC6500 locomotives were iconic in their day having been designed by the renowned Paul Arzens. They were the most powerful locomotives on the network at 8,000 hp and a small batch of them, including this locomotive, were temporarily fitted with third rail shoes for working heavy freight trains over the Maurienne line between Chambéry and Modane before overhead catenary was installed. Their monomotor bogies were designed with gear selection for freight and passenger work.

CC7121 was built by Alsthom/MTE/Fives-Lille during 1953. It is pictured in turquoise livery at Miramas depot on 9 April 2014 and was withdrawn from service in 1999 for preservation. CC7107 attained a record speed of 207 mph (331 km/h) on test runs during 1955.

CC7141 was built by Alsthom/MTE/Fives-Lille during 1954. It is pictured in turquoise livery at Lyon Oullins workshops on 30 July 1987 and was withdrawn from service during 1995.

CC14126 was built by Alsthom/Fives/CEM during 1955. It is pictured in green livery at Thionville depot on 14 November 1994 and was withdrawn from service during 1997. CC14100s were the dinosaurs of the heaviest freight traffic in the Lorraine region, having the same tractive effort as a British Rail Class 60 locomotive. However, their maximum speed of 36 mph was a limiting factor, which led to their withdrawal in the 1990s.

CC14131 was built by Alsthom/Fives/CEM during 1955. It is pictured in green livery at Thionville depot on 14 November 1994 and was withdrawn from service during 1997.

CC14200 was built by Alsthom/Fives/CEM during 1957. It is pictured in green livery at Metz Woippy yard on 15 November 1994 and was withdrawn from service during 1995.

CC14201 was built by Alsthom/Fives/CEM during 1957. It is pictured in green livery at Forbach depot on 14 November 1995 and was withdrawn from service during 1995.

CC40101 was built by Alsthom during 1964. It is pictured in stainless-steel livery at La Chapelle depot on 15 May 1992 and was withdrawn from service during 1995.

CC40106 was built by Alsthom during 1969. It is pictured in stainless-steel livery at La Chapelle depot on 15 May 1992 and was withdrawn from service during 1995.

CC65001 was built by Alsthom/CAFL/SACM during 1957. It is pictured in blue livery at Mohon depot on 17 November 1994 and was withdrawn from service during 1988 for preservation.

CC72007 was built by Alsthom/SACM/SEMT during 1968. It is pictured in blue livery at Lyon Vénissieux depot on 30 July 1987 and was withdrawn from service during 2004. CC72000s were iconic in their day, having been designed by Paul Arzens. They were the most powerful diesel locomotives on the network at 3,500 hp and the fastest at 100 mph. Their monomotor bogies were designed with gear selection for freight and passenger work.

CC72033 was built by Alsthom/SACM/SEMT during 1970. It is pictured in blue livery at Paris La Villette depot on 16 November 1994 and was withdrawn from service during 2011.

CC72050 was built by Alsthom/SACM/SEMT during 1970. It is pictured in blue livery at Lyon Vénissieux depot on 30 July 1987 and was withdrawn from service during 2005.

CC72074 was built by Alsthom/SACM/SEMT during 1972 and is pictured in blue livery at Châlons sur Marne depot on 13 November 1994.

CC72163 was built by Alsthom/SACM/SEMT during 1971. It is pictured in En Voyage livery at Chalindrey depot and was withdrawn from service during 2016.

Diesel and diesel shunting locomotives stabled around the roundhouse at Chalindrey depot on 13 November 1994.

Diesel and electric locomotives stabled outside the closed depot at Châlons sur Marne on 13 November 1994.

Above and below: Chambéry depot was the largest fully enclosed roundhouse with a glass dome that was ever built in France, measuring 110 metres in diameter and holding seventy locomotives on thirty-six lines. It was built between 1906 and 1910, became a listed historic building in 1984 and was refurbished during 2011 at a cost of €5 million.

A BB26000 electric locomotive and a pair of Y8000 diesel shunting locomotives stabled inside the roundhouse at Chambéry depot on 2 September 2014.

BB8100, BB7200, BB22000 and CC6500 electric locomotives stabled around the turntable at Paris Charolais depot on 15 May 1992.

Inside the signalling control centre of Strasbourg Hausbergen yard on 10 May 2022.

The largely disused sidings at Strasbourg Hausbergen yard on 10 May 2022.

Above and below: The remains of the roundhouse at Strasbourg Hausbergen yard on 14 November 1993 with BB13052 awaiting preservation. By 10 May 2022 the roundhouse had virtually been overgrown with vegetation.

BB16000 electric locomotives undergoing maintenance at Paris La Chapelle depot on 15 May 1992.

BB63000 diesel locomotives stabled around the turntable at Paris la Plaine depot on 16 May 1992.

BB15000 and CC72000 electric and diesel locomotives stabled at Paris La Villette depot on 15 May 1992.

BB16500 and BB63000 electric and diesel locomotives stabled at the west end of Lens depot on 27 October 1991.

BB12000, BB16500 and BB63000 electric and diesel locomotives stabled at the east end of Lens depot on 27 October 1991.

The turntable and roundhouse at Longueau depot on 17 May 1992.

The closed roundhouse at Marseille Charles depot on 24 May 2013.

BB36300 electric locomotives stabled at Modane depot on 5 February 2020.

BB7200 and BB36300 electric locomotives stabled inside the roundhouse at Modane depot on 5 February 2020.

Y2200 and BB26000 diesel shunting and electric locomotive inside the roundhouse at Mohon depot on 17 November 1994 which has recently been purchased by a company that will manufacture special rolling stock.

Preserved X2100 and X2800 railcars stabled at the preserved roundhouse at Montluçon depot on 25 April 2016.

The roundhouse at Paris Montrouge depot on 26 October 1991.

Above and below: The roundhouse by night at Nevers depot on 20 September 2022. I have a very close affiliation with staff at this depot and was very sad to see its closure during December 2022. However, SNCF have been refused permission to demolish it and I look forward to visiting it again one day, hopefully housing preserved rolling stock.

BB67400 diesel locomotive under maintenance in the roundhouse at Nevers depot on 10 October 2021.

The roundhouse by day at Nevers depot on 14 January 2017.

The rear of the buildings of Lyon Oullins workshops on 30 July 1987.

Above and below: Paris Sud Ouest was one of the few depots that was equipped with a traverser and several BB300 and BB4200 electric locomotives are stabled behind it on 15 May 1992. Someone at the depot had a sense of humour when a BB4200 electric locomotive crashed through the wall and onto the busy road behind it. The wall graffiti suggests that on leaving the depot you give priority to vehicles from the right.

CC6500, BB7200 and BB8500 electric locomotives are stabled in and around the front of the heavy maintenance facility at Paris Sud Ouest depot on 16 November 1994.

BB36300 electric locomotives stabled at Saint Jean de Maurienne depot on 3 September 2014.

Condemned RRR coaching stock and a variety of electric and diesel locomotives stabled around the north end of Tours Saint Pierre de Corps depot on 2 July 2016.

Part of the vast marshalling yards complex at Tours Saint Pierre de Corps, much of which is now either empty or being used for the storage of freight wagons, on 2 July 2016.

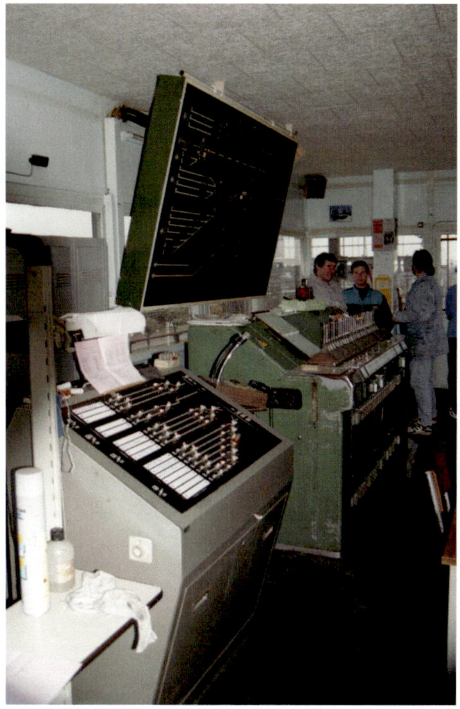

Above left: Ancient levers in an old manual signal box in Metz Woippy yard on 15 November 1994.

Above right: Inside the signalling control centre at Somaine yard on 18 November 1994.

Bogie gas tanks being hump shunted at Somaine yard on 18 November 1994.

Above and below: Rouen Sotteville yard became the cemetery for electric, diesel and diesel shunting locomotives, following the cessation of wagon load traffic and reduction in other freight services and locomotive-hauled passenger trains. When these pictures were taken on 29 April 2016, there were over 500 electric, diesel and diesel shunting locomotives stored surplus to requirements and SNCF received strong criticism from the media about the waste of rolling stock resources. As a result of this, many hundreds more stored locomotives remained at their depots until a new scrapyard was opened in Baroncourt, where most have been sent for disposal.

Strasbourg depot from the multistorey car park, where BB25000, BB26000 and BB67400 locomotives can be seen stabled on 27 August 2019.

A colourful picture of electric, diesel and diesel shunter locomotives with Alsace coaching in the background stabled around Strasbourg depot on 15 April 2015.

Above and below: Outside and inside the partially dismantled roundhouse at Thionville depot on 14 November 1994.

CC14100, BB25500 and Y7000 electric and diesel shunting locomotives stabled at the front of Thionville depot on 14 November 1994.

Right and below right: Toulouse is one of few depots that has both a traverser and turntable supplying to it, which maximises the storage and ease of access and egress of locomotives from within it. The close-up picture taken on 16 September 2015 shows how the traverser supplies the heavy maintenance facility in the background and the stabling point, tangential to it in the foreground, with locomotives to and from maintenance. The picture taken on 10 April 2014 shows how the turntable supplies the traverser and stabling point with locomotives. A diesel shunting locomotive is used to shunt the depot.

Toulouse depot on 3 July 2015 showing the geographic relationship between the heavy maintenance facility, traverser and stabling point.

Toulouse depot and stabling point viewed from the multistorey car park alongside the station on 22 May 2013.

The turntable and heavy maintenance facility at Lyon Vénissieux depot on 30 July 1987.

Diesel and diesel shunting locomotives around the turntable at Lyon Vénissieux depot on 30 July 1987.

Diesel shunting locomotives stabled around the turntable at Villeneuve Saint Georges depot on 18 May 1995.

Above and below: Villeneuve Saint Georges depot is one of the largest and busiest roundhouses in France. These pictures were taken on 26 October 1991 and show the variety of electric and diesel locomotives stabled, many of which have now been withdrawn from service.

The front of the roundhouse at Villeneuve Saint Georges depot showing the landscaping around it on 26 October 1991.

French and German electric locomotives stabled at Metz Woippy yard stabling point on 29 August 2019.

One of SNCF's busiest marshalling yards at Metz Woippy on 15 November 1994. This yard was used to facilitate the vast movement of freight in the Lorraine region, including coal, coke, steel and petrochemical products, both domestically and internationally to Germany, Luxembourg and Belgium.

Y2267, nearest to the camera, was built by Decauville during 1959. It is pictured in green livery at Béziers workshops on 29 July 1987 and was withdrawn from service during 1990.

Y2310 was built by Decauville during 1960. It is pictured in green livery at Lyons Vénissieux depot on 30 July 1987 and was withdrawn from service during 1990.

Y2453 was built by Decauville during 1965. It is pictured in green livery at Marseille Miramas depot on 9 April 2014 and was withdrawn from service during 1993.

Y5105 was built by De Dietrich during 1960. It is pictured in green livery at Paris Montrouge depot on 15 May 1992 and was withdrawn from service during 1993.

Y5116 was built by De Dietrich during 1960. It is pictured in green livery at Nevers depot on 14 July 2017 and was withdrawn from service during 1993. It was subsequently renumbered LOCMA0076 and is currently being used as an internal shunting locomotive at Nevers depot.

Y5155 was built by De Dietrich during 1961. It is pictured in green livery at Paris La Chapelle depot on 15 May 1992 and was withdrawn from service during 1993.

Y6323 was built by BDR during 1955. It is pictured in green livery at Mohon depot on 17 November 1994 and was withdrawn from service during 1993.

Y6327 was built by BDR during 1955. It is pictured in green livery at Chalindrey depot on 13 November 1994 and was withdrawn from service during 1987.

Y6509 was built by De Dietrich during 1956. It is pictured in green livery at Longueau depot on 17 May 1992 and was withdrawn from service during 1993.

Y7464 was built by Decauville during 1964. It is pictured in green livery at Paris La Plaine depot on 16 May 1992 and was withdrawn from service to be re-engineered into a Class Y9000 diesel shunting locomotive in around 2013.

Y8010 was built by Moyse/Fauvet Girel during 1977. It is pictured in orange and brown livery at Strasbourg Hausbergen yard on 25 April 2018 and was withdrawn from service during 2021.

Y8110 was built by Moyse/Fauvet Girel during 1980 and is pictured in orange and brown livery at Nevers depot on 10 October 2021.

Y8505 was built by Fauvet Girel during 1993 and is pictured in orange and brown livery at Chambéry depot on 2 September 2014.

Y9023 was re-engineered from Y7310 around 2011. It is pictured in Infra livery at Miramas depot on 9 April 2014.

Y9040 was re-engineered from Y7274 in around 2012 and is pictured in Infra livery at Chambéry depot on 2 September 2014.

Acknowledgements

I would like to dedicate this book to all the SNCF staff that have helped, encouraged and made it happen for me during the past forty years.

Special thanks to Charles Hinton, Alessandro Mimardo, Dominique Robin, Patrick Bernardi, Franck Nordman Montcharmont, Lionel Suty, Otta Rmn, Coco Lala, Thierry Poissenet, Guy Diebold and Florian Rocton.